Saint ⟨Thérèse of Lisieux⟩

⟨The⟩ Way of Love

Written by
Mary Kathleen Glavich, SND

Illustrated by
Virginia Esquinaldo

Pauline
BOOKS & MEDIA

Boston

Library of Congress Cataloging-in-Publication Data

Glavich, Mary Kathleen.
  Saint Thérèse of Lisieux : the way of love / written by Mary
Kathleen Glavich ; illustrated by Virginia Esquinaldo.
    p. cm. — (Encounter the saints series)
Summary: A biography of the nineteenth-century Christian saint,
Thérèse Martin, also known as Saint Thérèse of Lisieux.
  ISBN 0-8198-7074-9 (pbk.)
  1. Thérèse, de Lisieux, Saint, 1873–1897—Juvenile
literature. 2. Christian saints—France—Lisieux—Biography—
Juvenile literature. 3. Lisieux (France)—Biography—Juvenile
literature. [1. Thérèse, de Lisieux, Saint, 1873–1897. 2. Saints.
3. Women—Biography.] I. Esquinaldo, Virginia, ill. II. Title. III.
Series.
  BX4700.T5G57 2003
  282'.092—dc22

                                          2003013708

"P" and PAULINE are registered trademarks of the Daughters
of St. Paul

Text copyright © 2003, Sr. Mary Kathleen Glavich, SND
Illustrations and edition copyright © 2003, Daughters of St. Paul

Published in the U.S.A. by Pauline Books & Media, 50 Saint
Pauls Avenue, Boston, MA 02130-3491. www.pauline.org.
Printed in the U.S.A.

Pauline Books & Media is the publishing house of the Daughters
of St. Paul, an international congregation of women religious
serving the Church with the communications media.

3 4 5 6 7   13 12 11 10 09

Encounter the Saints Series

Blesseds Jacinta and Francisco Marto
Shepherds of Fatima

Blessed Pier Giorgio Frassati
Journey to the Summit

Blessed Teresa of Calcutta
Missionary of Charity

Journeys with Mary
Apparitions of Our Lady

Saint Anthony of Padua
Fire and Light

Saint Bakhita of Sudan
Forever Free

Saint Bernadette Soubirous
And Our Lady of Lourdes

Saint Edith Stein
Blessed by the Cross

Saint Elizabeth Ann Seton
Daughter of America

Saint Faustina Kowalska
Messenger of Mercy

Saint Frances Xavier Cabrini
Cecchina's Dream

Saint Francis of Assisi
Gentle Revolutionary

Saint Ignatius of Loyola
For the Greater Glory of God

Saint Isaac Jogues
With Burning Heart

Saint Joan of Arc
God's Soldier

Saint John Vianney
A Priest for All People

Saint Juan Diego
And Our Lady of Guadalupe

Saint Katharine Drexel
The Total Gift

Saint Martin de Porres
Humble Healer

Saint Maximilian Kolbe
Mary's Knight

Saint Paul
The Thirteenth Apostle

Saint Pio of Pietrelcina
Rich in Love

Saint Teresa of Avila
Joyful in the Lord

Saint Thérèse of Lisieux
The Way of Love

For other children's titles on the saints, visit our Web
site: www.pauline.org.

Contents

1

THE LITTLE QUEEN

Thirteen-year-old Marie Martin and her eleven-year-old sister Pauline couldn't sleep. Their mother was in her room having her ninth child.

"Marie," whispered Pauline, "do you think the baby will be a boy or a girl?"

Marie sat up. "I hope it's a boy," she replied. "Papa loves us four girls, but a boy would go fishing with him. On the other hand, Mama said she wants another girl like Thérèse." The last baby, Thérèse, had died shortly after birth. Three other Martin children had also died.

"Boy or girl, I just hope this baby lives," Pauline sighed.

"You know," mused Marie, "if Mama and Papa hadn't married, none of us would be here. They both wanted to join religious communities, but it didn't work out."

"I know the story," said Pauline, leaning on her elbow. "Mama met Papa on the bridge and knew he was the one for her. She was twenty-six and he was thirty-five. She made and sold lace, and he was a watch-maker and jeweler. Mama convinced him that they were meant for each other. They got married and lived happily ever after . . . with us!"

"Yes, with us!" agreed Marie. After a few moments she added, "Too bad the baby didn't come yesterday, on New Year's Day."

"It doesn't matter, Marie. Our new little brother or sister is going to *make* our life new!"

"You're right about that," Marie whispered excitedly. "And I'm going to be the godmother! I wonder what the baby will be like?"

"I'm sure that your godchild will be as good as Mama and Papa. How many other couples get up early every morning to go to Mass? Don't worry!"

"Pauline, do you think the baby will be dark like us and Celine, or fair like Leonie?"

"We'll soon find out."

"Well, we'd better get to sleep, or we won't be our best to meet our brother or sister in the morning. Good night, Pauline."

"Good night, Marie."

A little before midnight Louis Martin entered the older girls' room. "Pauline, Marie," he gently called. "Wake up."

"Is the baby here, Papa?" Pauline sleepily asked.

"Yes!" Mr. Martin whispered happily. "You have a sister. We're going to name her Marie-Francoise-Thérèse, but we'll call her Thérèse. Your mother's fine. You can visit them both in the morning." Before the girls could squeal in excitement, Mr. Martin put his finger to his lips. "Shh," he cautioned. "We don't want to wake your two little sisters. They'll find out tomorrow. Now go back to sleep." He pulled the blankets up over his oldest daughters, kissed them, and tiptoed out.

On January 4, 1873, Thérèse was taken through the snow to be baptized at the Church of Notre Dame. She was clothed in the beautiful lace garment her mother had made. Then Thérèse was brought back to her home in the town of Alençon, which is in Normandy, northern France.

But Mr. and Mrs. Martin's happiness soon turned to concern. Several weeks after her birth, Thérèse became sick. Mrs. Martin couldn't nurse her to give her the milk she needed. One morning while Mr. Martin was on a trip, Mrs. Martin walked two miles to Rose Taille's house. When Mrs. Taille opened the door, Mrs. Martin begged, "Rose, please come! My baby is very sick. Would you nurse her as you did my two boys? Please?"

Mrs. Taille's husband appeared in the doorway. "Zelie," he said, "you know that Rose has children of her own. She can't go with you. I'm sorry."

"But Thérèse will die without her help!" Mrs. Martin pleaded.

"I'll come at once," said Mrs. Taille quietly.

By the time the women reached the Martin home, Thérèse looked lifeless. Mrs. Taille took her little body into her arms to feed her, while Mrs. Martin, crying, ran to her room to pray. When Mrs. Martin returned, Thérèse had drunk a little milk but was unconscious. She was so pale that her mother thought she had died. Suddenly the baby opened her eyes and smiled.

"This one will live, Zelie!" Mrs. Taille exclaimed. "I'll see to it."

Mrs. Taille took Thérèse into her home and fed her for fifteen months. When she worked in the fields, she put Thérèse in a wheelbarrow lined with hay. Sometimes Mrs. Taille tied Thérèse onto the back of Red Lady, her cow (so named because of the dark red spots on its white coat). Finally

Thérèse was healthy enough to go back to her own mother.

When Thérèse returned to her family, she was a sturdy, happy child, who talked, laughed, and ran about. Mrs. Martin wrote to her brother Isidore in Lisieux and to Marie and Pauline at boarding school: "Thérèse is a little imp. When she says 'no' nothing can make her give in. One could put her in the cellar a whole day and she'd sleep there rather than say 'yes.' But still she has a heart of gold." With her blond curls, merry gray eyes, and constant smile, Thérèse was the darling of the Martin family, especially of her father.

Mr. Martin nicknamed his girls. Marie was Diamond, Pauline was Lovely Pearl, Leonie was Brave Lady, and Celine was Valiant Lady. Thérèse he called Little Queen. Mr. Martin hung a swing in the yard. Tied onto it, Thérèse demanded, "Higher! Higher!" Another of her favorite activities was to sit on her father's boot as he walked around the house and garden. After Mr. Martin bought a small house with a large garden, the children enjoyed going there. Best of all Thérèse loved their Sunday walks. Her mother didn't work that day and joined them. On these walks they saw wheat fields, trees, and various flowers. Nature fascinated Thérèse and lifted her heart to God.

Surrounded by the love of her parents and sisters, Thérèse loved them fiercely in return. She was particularly fond of Celine, who was three years older. Thérèse couldn't bear to be separated from her.

Thérèse also had a special love for Pauline, whom people said would become a nun. Thérèse didn't know what that meant, but she told herself, *Then I will be a nun, too.*

One day Marie brought a string of beads home from school. "Look," she said to six-year-old Celine, "my teacher gave us these to help us do good deeds. Whenever you do something kind, or make a sacrifice—something that's hard for you—you push up a bead."

"Let me see," said Thérèse. She watched Marie push up a bead.

"When you practice self-control, like giving in to someone else during a game," Marie explained, "you keep track on these beads. Here, Celine, these are for you," Marie said, handing her the beads.

Always trying to imitate Celine, Thérèse broke in, "I want beads, too!" Marie drew another set from her pocket. "I brought beads for both of you," she said with a smile.

Thérèse kept her virtue beads in her pocket. She and Celine raced to see who would have the most beads up each day. Thérèse, who had temper tantrums, now practiced self-control. She usually won the bead contests.

Although only three years old, Thérèse had a sensitive conscience. If she misbehaved, the house echoed with her sobs. She quickly told on herself and asked forgiveness. An intelligent girl, Thérèse began to read at this age.

In May Mrs. Martin turned a room into a chapel and set her statue of Mary in it. Thérèse delighted in decorating it with flowers. One Sunday she had gathered flowers on the family walk. On her way to put them in the little chapel, she met her grandmother.

"Hello, Thérèse, did you have a nice walk?" her grandmother asked.

"Oh, yes, Grandmother," Thérèse replied.

"What pretty flowers you have there," remarked her grandmother.

"I picked them myself," said Thérèse proudly.

"I would like to have those flowers for my May altar," her grandmother remarked. "Would you give them to me as a present?"

Thérèse looked startled. Then she nodded. One by one she plucked the flowers out of her bouquet and handed them over. When they were all gone, Celine saw tears in Thérèse's eyes.

"Thank you, dear," said Thérèse's grandmother, and she left with the bouquet.

The Martin house was a happy place for Thérèse in those days. Her mother ran her lace-making business from home. It became so successful that Mr. Martin sold his own watch repair business in order to manage his wife's affairs. The Martins were a good, well-to-do Catholic family. It seemed that they had no problems.

But sorrow was about to enter the picture.

2
DIFFICULT CHANGES

At Christmas in 1876 Mrs. Martin learned that she had cancer. It was too late to operate on the tumor in her breast. Zelie prayed and made a pilgrimage to Lourdes, hoping for a cure. When the cure was not received, she faced death bravely. She spoke cheerfully of going to heaven and prepared her two oldest daughters to care for the family. She wrote to Pauline about her youngest two, "You and Marie will be able to raise them perfectly. Celine never commits the smallest deliberate fault. The little one will be all right too…. She has a spirit about her which I have not seen in any of you." Mrs. Martin continued lace making as long as possible.

During Zelie's last weeks, a neighbor came each morning to take Thérèse and Celine for the day. Finally the girls were brought to their mother's room. They knelt around her bed. Mr. Martin sobbed while a priest gave Zelie the Anointing of the Sick. Back then this sacrament was given only to someone who was dying. Two days later, when Thérèse was four and a half years old, her mother died. In those days, the wake was held at home.

"Come, Thérèse, kiss your mother for the last time," Mr. Martin sadly invited, lifting Thérèse so that she could kiss Mrs. Martin's forehead. Later, Thérèse stood for a long time staring at the lid of her mother's coffin that stood propped against a wall.

After the funeral the five girls, wearing black dresses, were together at home. A woman who had looked after the younger girls commented, "Poor little things, you have no mother now!"

At that, Celine ran to Marie exclaiming, "You will be my mother!" About to imitate her, Thérèse realized that Pauline might be hurt. So she turned to Pauline and said, "And you will be *my* mother!"

In the meantime Mrs. Martin's brother Isidore and his wife Celine were speaking with Mr. Martin. They knew that at the age of fifty-four, he was a gentle, dreamy person who would need help raising five daughters.

"Louis, Celine and I have been talking," said Isidore. "We think you should sell your business and move to Lisieux."

"Yes, Louis," seconded Celine. "Our two girls are close in age to your youngest. It would be a joy to have your girls nearby."

"Why don't I look for a house for you when I return?" asked Isidore.

"You're probably right," Mr. Martin replied. "What will I do without Zelie? She was my world. She ran our home. Yes, please look for a house."

"I'm also willing to become the legal guardian of your children, Louis," added Isidore.

"Thank you," Mr. Martin quietly answered, his white head bent and his eyes filled with tears.

In less than three months the Martin girls were on the train heading for Lisieux. Mr. Martin remained behind in Alençon to take care of business. Uncle Isidore met the children at the station and took them to his house for the night. The next morning they went to their new home, less than half a mile away.

"Oh, how pretty!" exclaimed Celine on seeing the pink brick and white stone house.

"It's larger than our old home," added Marie, possibly thinking that there would be more rooms to clean.

"I'm glad it has big trees and a garden," said Thérèse.

"There's a garden in the back, too," Uncle Isidore pointed out.

Trees and shrubbery edged the property. So when Mr. Martin joined the girls and asked, "What shall we call our new home?" the family decided on "The Little Bushes."

Mrs. Martin's death had changed Thérèse. Before she had been lively and outgoing. Now she became shy and very sensitive, crying easily. In her grieving father, Thérèse found a good companion. As a five-year-old, she would go to the little tower room on the roof where Mr. Martin withdrew to read, write, and pray, and she would stay with him. The two would walk the streets together. Tom, their white spaniel, trotted along. Strangers stopped and commented on Thérèse's striking blond hair. Every day the father and daughter visited one of the nearby churches.

Sometimes Thérèse accompanied Mr. Martin when he went fishing. She had a rod but didn't like to fish. Instead she liked sitting in the grass, watching the clouds and listening to far-off sounds. When Mr. Martin worked in the yard, Thérèse played there. She built tiny altars and manger scenes out of leaves, moss, and twigs. Some days she pretended to make tea.

"Here's some tea for you, Papa," she would say, handing him a teacup with bark in the bottom.

"Thank you, Little Queen," Mr. Martin would reply, pretending to sip the mixture. "Ah, delicious as always!"

In the evening when the family gathered, Mr. Martin would hold Thérèse on his lap and sing her old French songs. Then Pauline would put her to bed. Each night Thérèse would ask her "little mother," "Have I been good today? Is our Lord pleased with me?" If Pauline had answered no, Thérèse would have cried all night. To be good in God's eyes meant everything to her.

On Sundays the girls took turns having dinner at Uncle Isidore's. One night, Mr. Martin came for Thérèse at 8:00. Thérèse was glad that it was dark, for she loved the stars. As they were walking home, she suddenly noticed that the stars in the belt of the constellation Orion, the hunter, formed the letter T. Thérèse called out, "Papa, look! My name is written in heaven."

"Well, so it is," Mr. Martin agreed.

Thérèse grabbed her father's hand. "Lead me, please, Papa," she begged. And

"Papa, look! My name is written in heaven!"

she walked the rest of the way with head upturned, staring at the T in the sky.

The first time Thérèse saw the sea, she was impressed. Its majesty and power made her think of God. One evening Thérèse joined Pauline on a rock and watched the sunset.

"Look, Pauline," Thérèse said. "The sun is making a path of light across the water. It's like grace leading us to God. I'm like a little boat following the light to heaven."

When Thérèse was about six, she had a strange experience. It was a beautiful summer afternoon, and Mr. Martin was away. Gazing out the window at the garden, Thérèse saw a man who looked like her father. His head was covered by a thick veil, and he walked slowly. "Papa, Papa!" Thérèse excitedly called. But the person kept on walking and disappeared behind some fir trees.

At Thérèse's cry, Marie and Pauline rushed into the room. "Why are you calling Papa when he's not here?" Marie asked.

"A man in the garden looked like Papa," Thérèse explained, "but his head was covered."

"Maybe it was Victoire playing a trick," Marie suggested. (Victoire was their cook.)

But no, Victoire had not left the kitchen. The girls searched the garden but found no one. Years later when her father became mentally ill, Thérèse understood that the vision had been a prophecy.

This was the only unsettling event in Thérèse's young life at The Little Bushes. In the shelter of her home, Thérèse knew only love. School, though, was a very different world—one that Thérèse wasn't ready for.

3

SCHOOL DAYS

For four years Pauline taught and guided Thérèse, while Marie ran the house. Thérèse's "little mother" was wise and patient.

"Pauline, you said that everyone will be perfectly happy in heaven," Thérèse ventured one day. "But if each person gets a fair reward, won't good people be happier in heaven than those who were not as good on earth?"

"Bring me one of Papa's big glasses and one of your small ones," Pauline answered. Meanwhile she herself went and got a pitcher of water.

Pauline filled the two glasses with water. "Now," she asked, "which glass is completely filled?"

"They both are!" Thérèse replied, breaking into one of her beautiful smiles. "Now I understand. Each person in heaven will be as happy as they can be!"

When Thérèse was eight and a half, Mr. Martin decided that it was time for her to go to school at the Benedictine Abbey where Celine was a student. Every day the two sisters met their two cousins at Uncle Isidore's house and walked to school. Every day they walked home accompanied by a maid. The girls wore black uniforms and white bonnets, quite a change for Thérèse who was used to fine, fashionable clothes.

The Benedictine Sisters gave Thérèse a good education, but she suffered in school. When students acted up in class, Thérèse was shocked and didn't join in. This set her apart. Thérèse, who had been placed with older girls, was usually first in her class, although she found memorizing difficult. The chaplain even called her his "little Doctor of Theology," which meant a master of religion.

The older students, especially one fourteen-year-old, were jealous of Thérèse. "Here she comes, Miss Goody-Goody," they said, making sure she heard. "She's not really so smart. Every free day her big sisters help her with her schoolwork."

The taunts and tricks were painful for shy Thérèse who had never experienced meanness before. On the playground Thérèse was not good at games and didn't know how to play with other children. The girls made fun of her until she cried. She began to withdraw. Alone, she would bury a dead bird or pray the rosary. Her father rewarded her good grades with coins, which she saved for the poor. During most of her school career, Thérèse was lonely and humiliated, but she never told her family.

A teacher once asked her, "What do you do during your free time at home?"

"Sometimes I go and hide myself in a little corner of my room which I can shut off with my bed curtains, and...I just think," Thérèse replied.

"And what do you think about?" the sister asked, amused.

"About God," Thérèse said, "about how short life is, and about eternity." Thérèse was already being drawn to prayer.

One day Thérèse overheard Marie and Pauline talking about Pauline entering Carmel. This was a nearby monastery of cloistered Carmelite nuns. (Being "cloistered" meant that the nuns never left the monastery.) They spent their days and part of the nights in prayer. Thérèse was stunned at the news. She couldn't imagine that her "second" mother would be leaving her.

"Thérèse," Pauline explained, "the sisters at Carmel live for God alone. This is what I want to do with my whole heart. It will make me very happy."

As Thérèse thought over Pauline's words, a desire to enter Carmel was born in her heart. Soon after, she confided to Pauline, "I want to be a Carmelite, too."

One Sunday Pauline took Thérèse to meet the prioress, Mother Marie de Gonzague. The sisters spoke to outsiders only through a grille, a kind of screen that separated them from their visitors. The two girls sat on one side of the grille and Mother Marie de Gonzague on the other. When Thérèse was alone with the prioress she said, "I would like to enter Carmel with Pauline. On the day she is clothed with the habit, I'd like to make my First Communion."

Mother Gonzague replied, "Dear child, you may have a vocation, a call to be a Carmelite. However, our rule doesn't allow anyone to enter until the age of sixteen. You must wait."

Thérèse went home discouraged.

After Pauline entered Carmel, Thérèse saw her only during the family's visits to the monastery. She spent the few minutes she had with Pauline crying.

Thérèse held on to her dream of entering Carmel. One day she thought about her name as a sister. Maybe instead of getting a new name she could keep Thérèse and be called Sister Thérèse of the Child Jesus. On that same day her family visited Pauline. Suddenly Mother Marie de Gonzague said to Thérèse, "My dear little girl, when you come to us, you will be called Thérèse of the Child Jesus."

4

A STRANGE SICKNESS

Going to school became more and more difficult for Thérèse. She missed Pauline so much that she began having frequent headaches.

When Thérèse was ten years old, she came down with a mysterious illness. Her condition became serious when Mr. Martin was away with the older girls and Thérèse and Celine were staying at their Uncle Isidore's. One evening Thérèse and Uncle Isidore were alone. Uncle Isidore began to speak about his sister, Thérèse's mother, whom he loved. Thérèse started to cry hard. She couldn't stop. Severe headaches followed, and by evening Thérèse was shivering as though she had a fever.

When Mr. Martin returned he took Thérèse home and put her to bed. It was weeks before she got better. Sometimes she lay still for hours. Other times she had convulsions and threw herself onto the floor. She imagined she saw horrible things and screamed. Thérèse said later that she was always aware of what was happening. The doctors couldn't explain her condition. All their treatments did no good.

In April of 1883 Pauline was to receive the Carmelite habit in a ceremony resembling a wedding. Thérèse announced, "I'm going to Pauline's clothing." Everyone concluded that it would be impossible. But on the morning of the clothing, Thérèse appeared well and was able to attend. The next day she was so sick that her family feared she was dying. She didn't even recognize them anymore.

"Write to Paris and ask for a novena of Masses to be said for Thérèse at Our Lady of Victories Church," Mr. Martin instructed Marie.

In May Thérèse kept calling for her mother. When Marie came into the room, Thérèse didn't recognize her. Marie tried to give her something to drink. Terrified, Thérèse screamed, "You're trying to poison me!"

Mrs. Martin's statue of Mary was in Thérèse's room. In desperation Marie knelt before it and begged for help. Thérèse too gazed at the statue and prayed. As Thérèse watched, the statue became very beautiful and seemed to smile. The pain disappeared.

Tears flowed down Thérèse's cheeks. She knew she was cured. The next morning, after ten weeks of suffering, Thérèse was perfectly normal again.

A year later Thérèse made her First Communion. Marie, her godmother, helped instruct her. Pauline gave her a notebook to record virtues and sacrifices offered to prepare for the day. Leonie gave her a large crucifix, which she wore on her belt. As was the custom, a week before her First Communion, Thérèse moved into the Abbey boarding school for days of prayer and silence. The sisters helped her do her hair because Thérèse had never combed it herself before. Her sisters did everything for her at home.

When Thérèse first received Jesus in the Holy Eucharist, she was overjoyed and moved to tears. She prayed, "I love you, Jesus, and I give myself to you forever." That day she wrote resolutions: "I will never lose courage. I will say a Memorare [a prayer to Mary] every day. I will try to humble my pride."

During the next two years Thérèse suffered from a spiritual problem known as scruples. She became overly concerned about doing the right thing and was always afraid that she was sinning. Thérèse was determined to be a saint like the heroes she read about in historical novels—like St. Joan of Arc. She worried and cried whenever she thought she had done something wrong. She suffered from low self-esteem. Later, Thérèse would live and teach a kind of spirituality that is just the opposite of her thinking at this time. It's called the Little Way.

Marie helped Thérèse deal with her scruples. Mr. Martin took her out of school and sent her to a tutor twice a week. In the friendly atmosphere of the tutor's home, Thérèse gained self-respect. Her tutor's mother entertained visitors in the room where Thérèse studied.

"Who's the lovely young girl reading the book?" one woman asked.

"That's Thérèse Martin, whom my daughter is tutoring," replied the mother.

"What beautiful hair she has!" observed another visitor.

Flattered by these remarks, Thérèse was afraid of becoming proud of herself. To prevent this, she joined the Children of Mary, a group of women and girls who prayed, did good deeds, and sewed. Thérèse attended meetings at the Abbey twice a week but was too shy to make friends.

"I wish I could get to know Thérèse better," Joan said to Lisette one day.

"She just sits sewing by herself during our sessions," her friend replied.

"Some days I try to talk to her afterwards, but she disappears too quickly," Joan remarked with a frown.

"You know where she goes, don't you?" asked Lisette. "She kneels in chapel until her father comes for her."

When Thérèse was thirteen, her sister Leonie abruptly entered the Poor Clare convent. A week later, Marie joined Pauline at Carmel. Again Thérèse was overcome with grief. She began to pray to her four deceased brothers and sisters. She reasoned that they were already in heaven and could not be taken away from her. Although Thérèse prayed for peace, she felt so sad that she wished her life were over.

But something was about to happen that would change everything....

5

CHRISTMAS CONVERSION

At the time Thérèse lived, children in France received their presents on New Year's Day instead of on Christmas. On Christmas they set out their shoes, and these were filled with small gifts and candy. The year Thérèse was nearly fourteen, she placed her shoes out as usual.

That Christmas night of 1886 Mr. Martin and his three daughters came in from midnight Mass. (Leonie had already left the convent and returned home.) Brushing the snow from his coat, Mr. Martin spotted Thérèse's shoes, which Celine had filled with gifts, before the fireplace in the dining room.

"Thérèse ought to have outgrown this sort of thing by now. I hope this will be the last time," he mumbled under his breath.

Thérèse, on her way upstairs to put her things away, overheard the remark. The words cut her like a knife. Her heart was pounding. Celine, who was behind Thérèse, realized how hurt she was. Knowing that she cried for every little thing, Celine advised, "Don't go down just yet. You'll only cry if you open your presents now."

But, surprisingly, Thérèse was able to hold back her tears. "I'll be all right," she replied. She went downstairs, knelt by the fireplace and opened her gifts with as much delight as always. Celine couldn't believe her eyes! Mr. Martin's mood had also changed, and he enjoyed the whole experience, too.

Thérèse viewed the strength she exercised that night as a present from the Christ Child, a special grace. After that, she hardly ever cried. She was a new person, free from fear, self-pity, and sensitivity.

From then on, practicing virtue became easier for Thérèse. She took over some housework to help the maid. She also gave food to beggars at the door. Her favorite book became *The Imitation of Christ*.

The power of God's love, which Thérèse experienced that Christmas night, was something she would share with others from then on.

6
Winning a Heart

The Mass ended. Thérèse closed her missal, and a holy card of the crucifixion partially slipped out. Thérèse saw one of Jesus' hands nailed to the cross and bleeding. It struck her that his blood was shed for all, but some people didn't know this. She decided to try in every way possible to bring God's saving love to others. Thérèse began to discuss this desire of hers with others, beginning with the family's maid. She also began to pray in a special way for sinners.

One day when Mr. Martin and his daughters were at dinner he asked, "Do you remember that thief I told you about, the one who murdered two women and a little girl? His name was Pranzini."

"Yes, Papa," the girls nodded.

"Well, today he was condemned to death."

"Oh, how awful!" exclaimed Celine. "I bet he's sorry for those crimes."

"According to the newspapers, Pranzini's not sorry at all," Mr. Martin said quietly, passing the bread to Thérèse. "He's refused to see a priest even now that he's facing death."

Thérèse almost dropped the bread basket. "He won't go to heaven then, will he, Papa?" she asked.

"God is all-merciful, but he respects our free will, Thérèse," answered Mr. Martin. "The Lord won't force anyone to be sorry for his or her sins. Pranzini needs to decide whether or not he wants to be with God in heaven. If he's sorry for the terrible things he's done, God will surely forgive him."

To Thérèse, Pranzini was a prime example of a person who was wasting the precious blood that Jesus had shed on the cross. She began a campaign of prayer and sacrifice to help Pranzini reach heaven. She offered God all the merits of Jesus and all the Church's treasures for his conversion. Thérèse prayed, "My God, I am sure you are going to forgive this miserable Pranzini, and I have so much confidence in your mercy that I shall go on being sure even though he doesn't go to confession, or show any sign at all of being sorry. But because he is the first sinner I'm praying for, please give me just one sign to let me know."

Every day Thérèse hoped to learn that Pranzini was sorry for his sins. Finally the execution day arrived...and Pranzini hadn't changed his heart. The next day Thérèse skimmed the account of his execution in the paper. Even on the scaffold Pranzini had refused to ask forgiveness. Then, tied to the guillotine, Pranzini had said, "I want the crucifix." The chaplain had held the crucifix out to him, and Pranzini had kissed it three times.

Thérèse was so happy and grateful! Her prayers had helped this poor man obtain God's forgiveness. Thérèse called Pranzini her "first-born." Later on at Carmel, she even had Masses celebrated for him.

Thérèse's desire to bring many people closer to God continued to grow. So did her longing to become a nun.

But there were still many obstacles to come....

7

REVEALING THE CALL

Thérèse was determined to be a Carmelite. She wanted to pray and make sacrifices for others, and especially for priests. Visiting Carmel, she discussed her ambitions with Pauline and Marie.

"I want to live only for Jesus. I want to offer myself for the Church," Thérèse told her sisters. "Do you think I could enter this Christmas, the anniversary of my conversion?"

"Thérèse, I know how you feel," Pauline responded, "but you're not yet fifteen."

"I could get special permission," Thérèse countered.

"Yes, you could," said Pauline.

"No," Marie broke in. "That wouldn't be wise. You're too young. Our life is difficult. Wait five or six years."

"You are mature for your age, Thérèse," Pauline admitted. "If you pray, maybe our Lord will make an exception."

"Don't encourage her," Marie cautioned Pauline. "Thérèse, think of Celine. She's older than you and wants to join Carmel. Shouldn't you let her come first?"

"I've talked to Celine," Thérèse said. "She's willing to let me enter first."

"Have you considered what it would do to Papa if you, his Little Queen, would leave him now?" Marie argued. "Have you told him that you want to become a nun?"

"No," Thérèse admitted, "But I intend to soon. I'm sure he'll understand."

"Poor Papa," Pauline sighed. "He isn't himself since that stroke."

"He's sixty-four years old," Marie pointed out. "He's going to need care."

"Thérèse, since you're sure this is what God wants, I think you should try to enter the monastery now. I'll pray for you," Pauline promised.

Marie just shook her head at her impractical sisters.

Thérèse chose the feast of Pentecost to break her news to her father. It was a beautiful May evening in 1887. Mr. Martin was sitting on a bench in the garden, his hands loosely clasped. Thérèse approached and sat next to him without speaking.

Mr. Martin turned to her and saw her eyes filled with tears. Putting an arm around her and drawing her close, he asked,

"What's the matter, Little Queen? You can tell me." He stood and the two walked slowly down the path.

"Papa," Thérèse started out, "I wish to enter Carmel."

"Ah, I thought you would want to give your life to God," Mr. Martin nodded.

"But, Papa, I want to join *now*," Thérèse said, beginning to cry.

Mr. Martin hugged her harder, and Thérèse saw tears streaming down his face, too.

"You're very young to make such a serious decision," said Mr. Martin.

"I've wanted to give myself to God for years," explained Thérèse. "God has planted this desire in my heart so strongly that nothing else will make me happy. Remember when I was little and Leonie offered Celine and me a basket of ribbon, lace, and colorful fabric to choose from? Celine took silk braid, but I grabbed the whole basket and said, 'I choose everything!' You teased me about that. Well, I still want all. I desire the most special life. I want to spend my life for God praying for people."

"I believe you, my dear good daughter," Mr. Martin replied. "You have my permission. However, what the Church and Carmel say is another matter."

The two walked for some time. Then Mr. Martin bent to pluck a little white flower from a low stone wall. It came out with its roots intact. "God made this fragile little flower blossom and grow even though the slightest accident could have damaged it," he observed. He handed the flower to Thérèse.

Thérèse knew that the flower stood for her. Like it, she had grown in the Martin home and now could be safely transplanted to Carmel. Later Thérèse fastened the flower to a picture of Our Lady of Victories. She kept it until she died. Thérèse entitled the autobiography she later wrote "The Story of the Springtime of the Little White Flower."

The next hurdle for Thérèse on the journey to Carmel was Uncle Isidore, her legal guardian. The following Wednesday she visited him.

"Uncle Isidore," she began, "I would like to enter Carmel this year."

"What?" Uncle Isidore nearly shouted. "You're little more than a child and haven't even finished school. How can you speak of Carmel?"

"I know I'm young, but I could be an exception."

"Exception nothing!" Uncle Isidore exploded. "What you're suggesting is ridiculous, an insult to our Church."

"Papa said I may go," Thérèse ventured.

"Your father doesn't realize how this could harm you," an exasperated Uncle Isidore said.

"But, Uncle Isidore," Thérèse pleaded, "I'm sure God is calling me to Carmel."

"Not at your age. I forbid it," Uncle Isidore declared. "Only a miracle would change my mind."

Thérèse went home and for three long, rainy days prayed for a miracle. On Saturday she returned through the rain to her uncle's house.

"Thérèse," he greeted her, "you don't have to fear me. I've been praying about your request. God has let my heart know that you are to enter Carmel."

"Oh, Uncle Isidore, thank you!" Thérèse exclaimed.

"Go in peace, my dear child," he said as he embraced her. "You are a little flower that God has chosen and wishes to gather for himself. I won't stand in the way."

By the time Thérèse left, the sun was shining in a blue sky. It mirrored the happiness in her heart.

8

RESISTANCE

Mother Marie de Gonzague was ready to accept Thérèse. However, Father Delatro-ëtte, who supervised Carmel, was against it. He knew the demands of the Carmelite life. He also knew that Thérèse was a sheltered, pampered girl who had had a kind of nervous breakdown. When Mother Marie de Gonzague asked the priest if Thérèse could enter, he answered emphatically, "No, not until she's twenty-one!"

At one point the revered founder of the Carmelite community, Mother Genevieve, spoke to Father Delatroëtte on Thérèse's behalf. He merely growled, "You'd think the whole fate of Carmel depended on this girl!"

Then Thérèse and her father visited Father Delatroëtte. The priest held firm. He would not allow a fourteen-year-old to enter Carmel. In his eyes this would be foolish. As the Martins turned to go, however, the priest remarked, "I'm only the bishop's delegate, of course. If he gave you his permission to enter, I could not prevent it."

Immediately Mr. Martin wrote the bishop asking for an interview. Summer came and went before his request was granted. While waiting, Thérèse helped poor families and tutored two little girls whose mother was sick.

On October 31 Mr. Martin and Thérèse made the two-hour journey to the bishop's residence. To appear older, Thérèse wore her hair up for the first time. It was gathered under a ladylike hat. But she was not as confident as she looked. Although her shyness made her dread talking to the bishop, she would pay any price to obtain her goal. She hoped that this man of God would understand her desire and grant her permission.

Mr. Martin and Thérèse arrived at the bishop's house in the pouring rain. The two were escorted to a room where Father Révérony, the bishop's assistant, waited. "Come in," the priest said. His face betrayed his surprise at how young Thérèse was. She noticed this, and tears welled up in her eyes.

"Oh, those diamonds must not be shown to the bishop," Father Révérony remarked as a teardrop slipped down Thérèse's cheek. Embarrassed, she followed the priest to a huge room where three large armchairs stood before a fireplace. The bishop sat in one. Father gestured to the middle chair, big enough for four children, and said to Thérèse, "Please be seated here."

"Oh, no thank you," Thérèse replied.

"Show that you can obey," teased the priest. So Thérèse sat uncomfortably between the bishop and her father, while the priest sat in a regular chair.

"Thérèse," prompted her father, "tell the bishop why we're here."

Thérèse did her best to explain why she wanted to be a Carmelite and why she thought an exception could be made. Her father remained silent.

"How long have you had this desire?" the bishop inquired.

"A very long time, my Lord," Thérèse answered.

Father Révérony laughed and said, "Come now, it can't be as long as fifteen years!"

"That's true," Thérèse replied solemnly, "but it is not much less, for I have wished to give myself to God since I was three."

"You are only fourteen," said Father Révérony. "Why don't you wait a few years?"

"I agree," the bishop said. "Stay home with your father a while longer."

Then Mr. Martin spoke up. "If God is calling Thérèse—and I believe God is—she has my permission to go now. My daughters and I are going on a pilgrimage to Rome. I know that Thérèse will speak to the Holy Father if permission is not granted her before then."

"Mr. Martin," replied the bishop, "your willingness to sacrifice your daughter for God is admirable. And, Thérèse, your love of God is beautiful. Father Révérony will be making the pilgrimage, too. I'm sorry, but I can't make a decision about your entrance until I confer with Father Delatroëtte. After all, he is in charge of Carmel."

Realizing that her fate was in the hands of Father Delatroëtte who opposed her entrance, Thérèse burst into tears.

"There, there," said the bishop, patting Thérèse's shoulder. "Don't give up hope. I'll talk to Father Delatroëtte next week. In the meantime instead of weeping, look forward to going to Rome. It will make your vocation stronger. In Italy, you will receive my answer." The bishop stood and walked the visitors to the garden gate.

"How wonderful of you, Mr. Martin, to offer your daughter to Carmel," commented Father Révérony. "Not many fathers would do that."

"It seems that God is not willing to accept my sacrifice just yet," replied Mr. Martin. He turned to the bishop and with a rueful smile confided, "Thérèse even put her hair up today to look older."

Thérèse, more humiliated than ever, and still crying, didn't feel at all old, but rather like a little child!

9

To the Pope

In November Mr. Martin, Thérèse, and Celine joined others in Paris to make a pilgrimage in honor of the pope's fiftieth anniversary of ordination. There Thérèse visited the Church of Our Lady of Victories and understood clearly that it really was Mary who had cured her years before.

From Paris the pilgrims boarded a train for Rome. Mr. Martin, who loved to travel, was in his glory. His daughter Thérèse, though, was anxious to get the journey over with and settle down in Carmel! As the train traveled through Switzerland, Thérèse and Celine were glued to the window. They passed lovely Lake Lucerne, quaint villages, rushing waterfalls, and the majestic Alps. Thérèse exclaimed, "Oh, Celine, I hope I never forget what this looks like. It will remind me of God's greatness when I have little troubles in Carmel."

In Italy the pilgrims went sightseeing in Milan, Venice, Padua, Bologna, and Loreto.

Frequently Thérèse was aware that Father Révérony was studying her.

On their first day in Rome the pilgrims visited the Colosseum, where early Christians had been martyred for their faith in Jesus. "The original soil of this arena is buried about twenty-five feet down," their guide explained. "See those barriers? Behind them the earth is being excavated to the old level. A stone with a cross on it marks the spot where the martyrs died. But, it's too dangerous to go down there."

"How I wish we could touch that soil!" Celine said.

Thérèse eyed the barriers. "Look," she said. "I think we can. There's a way down." The two girls ran off and—despite their long dresses—slid under a barricade, scrambling down the pile of rubble.

When they reached the bottom, Thérèse said, "Let's find the stone marker!" They soon located it. Thérèse knelt and kissed the ground. She prayed, "Let me be a martyr, too."

During the next days the pilgrims visited the churches of Rome, the Roman Forum and the catacombs where the early Christians secretly celebrated the Eucharist and buried their dead. The visit with the Holy Father was scheduled for their last day.

When that day, a Sunday, dawned, it was raining. At eight o'clock in the morning the pilgrims attended a Mass celebrated by Pope Leo XIII. The Gospel read, "Fear not, little flock, for it has pleased the Father to give you the kingdom." *I know the kingdom of Carmel will be mine,* Thérèse thought.

Afterwards, the group was ushered into the audience hall to meet the pope. He was quite old and hard of hearing. Clothed in a white robe with a white cap and white shoes, he sat on an armchair. One by one Father Révérony presented the visitors. As Father announced each person's name, he or she knelt before the pope. The pilgrim kissed the pope's foot and his ring to show reverence for this man who represented Christ on earth. The pope took each visitor's hand, said a few words, and then gave the person a blessing and a medal.

When it was Mr. Martin's turn, Father Révérony commented, "Mr. Martin has two daughters who are Carmelites." The Holy Father smiled and gave Mr. Martin a special blessing. Thérèse stood waiting, garbed in a long black dress and lace mantilla, the attire for women at a papal audience. Father Révérony glanced at her and warned, "It is absolutely forbidden to speak to the Holy Father!" Thérèse looked at Celine, who whispered, "Speak!" Then it was her turn.

Thérèse knelt on the step before the Holy Father and kissed his foot. Then she seized the pope's hand and looked up at him through her tears.

"Holy Father," she implored, "I want to ask you a great favor." The pope bent toward her. "Holy Father," Thérèse continued in a shaky voice, "in honor of your jubilee, let me enter Carmel at fifteen."

The pope turned to Father Révérony and said, "I don't understand."

Trying hard to control his temper, Father Révérony explained, "Holy Father, this is a child who wants to be a Carmelite. The superiors are already handling the matter."

The pope turned back to Thérèse. "Well, my child," he said, "do what the superiors decide."

Desperate, Thérèse folded her hands on the pope's knees and pleaded, "Holy Father, if you say yes, everyone else will be willing."

"You will enter if it is God's will," he answered.

"Holy Father, let me enter Carmel…"

Thérèse didn't move. She was not about to end the conversation. Two Swiss guards had to lift her and lead her away. The Holy Father raised his hand to bless the sobbing Thérèse.

That night Thérèse wrote Pauline, "God has given me courage to bear this trial, but it is very great. But, Pauline, I am the little plaything of the Child Jesus, and if he wants to break his toy, he is very welcome."

10

VICTORY!

The next day the pilgrims traveled to Naples and Pompeii. Mr. Martin stayed in Rome to visit the head of a college there. Coincidentally, Father Révérony was visiting the same college. Already he was somewhat ashamed of how he had treated Thérèse.

"Ah, Father Révérony," said Mr. Martin. "Remember how you had promised to help my daughter? You weren't much help yesterday..."

"Now that I know her, I think I may have been wrong," the priest admitted. "I'll be there for her clothing with the Carmelite habit," he promised, smiling. "I will invite myself to the ceremony!"

On the way home from Pompeii, the pilgrims visited the church of St. Francis and the monastery of St. Clare in Assisi. As they left, Thérèse realized she had lost her belt buckle. She ran back to the monastery and found it. But by the time she returned to the carriages, only one was left—Father Révérony's! Thérèse found herself seated across from him. Sensing her discomfort, the priest kindly assured her, "I will leave nothing undone that can help you to enter the monastery at fifteen."

Back at home in Lisieux, Mr. Martin knew his youngest daughter was suffering. One day he said, "How would you like to go with me to the Holy Land?"

"Thank you, Papa," Thérèse replied, "but I have seen enough of the world. All I want is to be in Carmel."

Thérèse still hoped to enter the monastery that Christmas. When she visited Marie and Pauline to tell them about the pilgrimage and the visit to the pope, she asked, "What should I do?" Pauline said, "Write to the bishop and remind him that he promised you an answer. Ask if you may enter at Christmas."

Thérèse wrote a letter with Uncle Isidore's help. Every day she eagerly checked the mail for a response. Christmas came and went. Then on New Year's Day, while visiting with Pauline, Thérèse heard good and bad news.

Three days after Christmas, Mother Marie de Gonzague had received a letter from the bishop authorizing her to accept Thérèse. However, Mother Marie de Gonzague decided that it would be better for Thérèse to enter after Lent. Thérèse's heart sank. She was not told that this decision was made to avoid insulting Father Delatroëtte. Furthermore, Pauline felt that it wouldn't be wise for Thérèse to undergo the strict Lenten penances of the Carmelites. Being a nun was difficult. Leonie had just returned home from the convent after another try.

The following day Thérèse turned fifteen. For the next three months she prepared for Carmel by practicing self-control and acts of kindness for others.

11

A DREAM COME TRUE

On April 9, 1888, which that year was the Feast of the Annunciation, Thérèse entered Carmel. Her yes to God echoed Mary's yes.

The day before entering, Thérèse went to Mass at her parish church for the last time. That evening Uncle Isidore and his family came to dinner. On April 9, Thérèse woke up early, put on a soft, blue woolen dress, and said goodbye to her house and garden. Then she walked to Carmel and waited, kneeling in the chapel. Behind the altar a grille separated the cloistered nuns from the public. The Martins and Uncle Isidore's family joined Thérèse for Mass. During Mass Thérèse could hear sobbing, but she herself didn't cry.

After Mass the large door into the cloister opened. Thérèse hugged her family members. Turning to her father, she knelt. "Papa, please give me your blessing," she begged. Crying, Mr. Martin knelt too. Facing his Little Queen, he traced the Sign of the Cross on her forehead. Then Thérèse rose and walked through the door. On the other side twenty-six sisters greeted and embraced her, beginning with her beloved Pauline and Marie. Their religious names were Sister Mary Agnes of Jesus and Sister Mary of the Sacred Heart.

One thing spoiled the day. Father Delatroëtte, a poor loser, stated sharply within earshot of Thérèse's family, "Reverend Mother, you may sing a Te Deum. As the bishop's delegate, I present you this child of fifteen whose entrance you desired. I hope she will not disappoint your expectations, but remember, if it should be so, you alone bear the responsibility." Those cruel words must have hurt her, but Thérèse didn't show it. She was at peace.

Mother Marie de Gonzague took Thérèse on a tour of the monastery. Then Thérèse was taken to her cell, her three-yard wide bedroom. It had a bare floor, a narrow window, a low cot with a straw mattress, a wooden bench, an earthen bowl and pitcher, and a stand to hold writing materials or a workbasket. On one white wall was a plain wooden cross without an image of Jesus.

Thérèse put the postulant cape on over her dress and covered her hair with the black bonnet. She would wear this outfit until she became a novice. Alone and looking out of the window, Thérèse was overcome with gratitude and joy. She repeated over and over, "Now I am here forever!"

But not everyone was so sure.

12

EARLY TESTING

The order that Thérèse joined was strict. The sisters prayed and did penance in order to draw close to God and help people reach heaven. After rising at five or six o'clock, the Carmelites spent time in silent prayer. Mass followed. The nuns met to pray the Divine Office together morning, noon, and night. Except for two hours of recreation every day when they sewed, the sisters didn't speak. Silence made it easier to converse with God. This meant that Thérèse did not speak to her sisters Pauline and Marie except in a group.

Dressed in heavy, coarse habits, the Carmelites worked five hours a day. Their work included cooking, sewing, housecleaning, laundry, nursing the sick sisters, and, in the summer, haying. Manual labor was a challenge for Thérèse who rarely had to work at home. She wasn't very good at it!

The nuns also practiced penance. For example, they would kneel on the floor with arms outstretched in the form of a cross, or they would beg for a meal. These practices were usual in religious communities at that time. The nuns fasted almost seven months of the year and never ate meat. During meals they listened to spiritual reading. The Carmelites lived a life of poverty and obedience to the prioress. Love of God gave them the strength to live this way. Despite their hard life, the nuns were happy.

Thérèse found the life difficult. What's worse, during her prayer time, she didn't feel close to God. Her mind wandered. The prayer position, kneeling or sitting on her heels, was uncomfortable, and she was often sleepy.

Besides all this, Mother Marie de Gonzague, whom Thérèse loved and admired, seemed to have turned against her. Actually the prioress wanted to test Thérèse's vocation, her self-control and endurance, and to help her grow in humility. When the prioress met with Thérèse to give her spiritual advice, she spent most of the hour scolding her.

One day after Thérèse had swept, Mother Marie de Gonzague noticed a spider web in a corner. Perhaps Thérèse's fear of spiders had led her to overlook this web. When the community was gathered, Mother Marie de Gonzague called, "Thérèse, come here."

Thérèse stood before all the sisters.

"It is easy to see that our cloisters are swept by a child of fifteen," Mother Gonzague announced. "What a pity! Go and sweep away that cobweb and be more careful in the future."

"Yes, Mother," Thérèse replied, her red face burning. She knelt and kissed the floor, which was the custom after committing a fault.

The novice director in charge of Thérèse's formation sent her outside to weed the garden every afternoon. Because going outside at this time was an exception, Thérèse felt uncomfortable doing it, especially because she usually met Mother Marie de Gonzague on her way out. One day when Thérèse encountered her, the prioress remarked, "Why, this child does absolutely nothing! What are we to think of a novice who needs a walk every day?"

Again, thinking that Thérèse needed more sleep, the novice director ordered, "Thérèse, for the next fifteen days, you are to stay in bed and rest. Don't come to morning prayer." Thérèse obeyed only to hear Mother Marie de Gonzague criticize, "So the young lady is getting herself coddled!"

Thérèse wasn't old enough to fast. Meals were penance anyhow. Thérèse was supposed to eat everything that was dished out on her plate. Some food didn't agree with her, especially when the cook was in a bad mood and served her spoiled leftovers. The novice director told Thérèse to tell her whenever she had a stomach ache. When Mother Marie de Gonzague heard that Thérèse was reporting a stomach ache almost daily, she commented, "For goodness' sake, that child is always complaining." She didn't know that Thérèse had been told to report this.

Thérèse accepted the unfair criticisms without a word and only spoke of them to her novice director. She never mentioned them to her two sisters. In fact, she kept at a distance from them so as not to take comfort in their affection. During recreation, when the nuns talked, Thérèse purposely sat with the sisters she was least attracted to.

A certain Jesuit, Father Pichon, understood Thérèse's holiness. One day she asked him, "Would you be my spiritual director?"

"My child," the priest replied, "may our Lord be always your Superior and your Novice Master."

Father Pichon was soon transferred to Canada, leaving Thérèse to be directed only by Jesus. She once exclaimed to another priest, "Oh, Father, I want to become a saint. I want to love God as much as St. Teresa of Avila did." St. Teresa had reformed the Carmelite order.

Behind Thérèse's back Mother Marie de Gonzague said, "She's the best among my best, a real angel." Despite Thérèse's obvious holiness, when it came time for her to become a novice, she was told, "It would be better if you had three more months as a postulant." Perhaps this was because Father Delatroëtte was still in charge. Another reason for the delay was that Mr. Martin had had another paralyzing stroke. The ceremony in which Thérèse would receive the Carmelite habit and become a novice would be the last time that she would leave the cloister and embrace her father. Delaying the ceremony would give Mr. Martin time to get well.

Thérèse accepted this decision. During these three winter months, she suffered from the cold. The community room, where the sisters had recreation, was the only heated room in the monastery. The rest of the convent was cold and damp. Sometimes Thérèse shivered all night in her cell. She offered her suffering as a sacrifice to God.

During these days Thérèse's love of Scripture grew. She always carried with her a small copy of the Gospels. Her understanding of Scripture amazed the other sisters.

"She's so young. Where does she get such wisdom?"

They wondered.

13

SISTER THÉRÈSE OF THE CHILD JESUS

January 9, 1889 was the date finally set for Thérèse's reception of the habit. She had decided to add to her name. Attracted by the image of the human face of the suffering Jesus, she wanted to be known as Sister Thérèse of the Child Jesus of the Holy Face.

Thérèse made a retreat to prepare for her clothing. During it she had no wonderful feelings while she prayed. Her prayer was dry. She complained, "I strive to find Jesus, and I find nothing."

Still, Thérèse looked forward to the ceremony and wrote to Pauline, "I wish to give all to Jesus, since he has made me understand that he alone is perfect happiness. All—all will be for him!" Then came another disappointment. Because of a funeral, the bishop could not preside over the ceremony until the following day.

Secretly, Thérèse hoped for snow for her clothing day. The weather, though, was spring-like. According to the custom of the nuns, Thérèse was first dressed as a bride. She wore a gown of white velvet trimmed with lace. Her veil was crowned with a wreath of lilies. Thérèse walked slowly to her family gathered in the outer chapel. Mr. Martin, who was well enough to attend the celebration, took her arm. "Ah, here is my little Queen," he happily sighed. He led Thérèse to the altar for Mass. Once, when questioned about his sacrifice of his youngest daughter, he had exclaimed, "If I had anything better to give to God, I would present it!"

After Mass, Thérèse, carrying a lighted candle, knelt before her father. The bishop began the Te Deum, a hymn of praise sung at vow ceremonies, not clothings. A priest whispered, "Bishop, the Magnificat is to be sung," but the bishop waved him away and continued with the Te Deum.

A second favor was granted to Thérèse this day. Walking back to the cloister for the rest of the ceremony, she discovered that the courtyard was blanketed with snow!

The bishop continued the ritual. He asked Thérèse, kneeling before him, "What do you desire?"

The cloister courtyard was blanketed with snow!

Thérèse responded, "The mercy of God, the poverty of the order, and the company of the sisters."

"Is it of your own free will that you wish to take the religious habit?"

"Yes," Thérèse answered.

"Do you wish to enter this order for the sole love of our Lord?"

"Yes," she said again, "by the grace of God and with the prayers of the sisters."

Then Thérèse went back into the monastery where her lovely blond hair was cut. She donned the Carmelite habit: the novice's white veil, brown serge robe, and rope-soled sandals. She was only sixteen years old.

Thérèse would not be the last Martin girl to enter the convent. Celine had informed their father that she too wanted to be a Carmelite, and Leonie intended to enter another cloistered community, the Visitation Nuns. Mr. Martin would give *all* his daughters to God.

14

SMALL THINGS

Sadly, Mr. Martin's health continued to deteriorate. He began to hallucinate. Thérèse often wrote to Celine, his caretaker, to encourage her. One day, thinking that his house was being attacked in a battle, Mr. Martin took up a gun. Uncle Isidore Guerin and a strong friend of his managed to disarm him. The doctor then committed Mr. Martin to a mental institution. His daughters were filled with grief.

Thérèse longed at times to be a martyr like Joan of Arc, and her father's illness became a real part of her "martyrdom." She wanted to be a missionary, even a priest. Eventually she realized that her path to heaven would be much simpler. God was calling her to be holy by doing ordinary things with extraordinary love. She was to be humble and forgotten, and she was to accept the sufferings that came to her with love. As a novice, Thérèse practiced virtue in little ways.

She practiced poverty because Jesus had lived a poor and simple life. One day a pretty little jug in her cell was replaced with a large chipped jug. Thérèse didn't complain. One evening the lamp she used disappeared. Thérèse remained in the dark rather than disturb the great silence kept at night.

Thérèse practiced love. One sister constantly irritated her. Thérèse told herself, *I will do for this sister the things I would do for the person I love most.* After awhile, the troublesome nun asked, "Sister Thérèse of the Child Jesus, tell me what is it about me that attracts you? Every time we meet, you greet me with a most gracious smile."

During silent prayer in chapel, the sister behind Thérèse kept tapping her fingernails against her teeth. This habit annoyed Thérèse so much that she couldn't pray. Although she was tempted to turn and stare at the sister, she simply listened to the clicking.

One gruff, elderly nun was crippled. "Sister St. Pierre," Thérèse offered, "I'd be glad to help you get to the dining room every evening." After that, each evening before leaving the chapel Sister St. Pierre shook her hourglass to signal "Let's go." Thérèse carried the sister's bench exactly as she was instructed. Slowly the two walked, with Thérèse holding the elderly nun's belt. Sometimes Sister St. Pierre stumbled. Then she'd mumble, "You're not holding me right!" At other times she'd complain, "Ah! Good heavens! You're going too fast. I'm going to break something." When Thérèse walked slower, the nun would grumble, "Well, come on! I don't feel your hand. You've let me go and I'm going to fall! I was right when I said you were too young to help me." After Thérèse got Sister St. Pierre settled at the table, she even cut her bread for her before smiling goodbye.

Thérèse practiced self-control. Speaking to Pauline and Marie would have comforted her, especially during their father's long illness. Yet Thérèse wouldn't ask permission to do this.

Only once as a novice did Thérèse have a supernatural favor. When she was praying the Stations of the Cross in the garden, God allowed her to experience a great joy like the joy of heaven. It lasted a week. Then Thérèse returned to her usual state of spiritual dryness.

Ordinarily a novice made vows after spending a year in the monastery. In Thérèse's case, Father Delatroëtte would not allow it. She had to wait nine more months.

Disappointed, Thérèse decided to use the time to prepare for her vows by practicing even more virtue. She compared these virtues to precious stones that would decorate her spiritual wedding gown on the day she would be consecrated to God.

15

VOW DAY

"Sister Marie of the Angels," Thérèse whispered to her novice director in chapel. "I must see you!"

It was the night before Thérèse was to make her vows. She was completing a ten-day retreat. Sister Marie saw the distress on Thérèse's face, rose, and left the chapel with her. When they got to her office, Sister Marie invited her, "Dear child, sit down. What's wrong?"

"Sister," Thérèse said, "I've just realized that although the life of Carmel is beautiful, it's not for me. I've made a mistake. I've misled all of you."

"What makes you think this?" Sister Marie probed.

"It seems that being a Carmelite was just a dream I had. God's not really calling me. It's foolish of me to think so," Thérèse said in a low voice.

"My, the devil's having fun with you!" Sister Marie exclaimed with a laugh. "Listen, during your years with us, haven't you been happy?"

"Of course. I've had deep joy," Thérèse admitted.

"That's the sign of a vocation," Sister Marie pointed out. Smiling, she continued, "We sisters and even Father Delatroëtte have invited you to make your vows. Do you think we are *all* wrong in judging that you will be a good Carmelite?"

"No," said Thérèse thoughtfully.

"You're just like a bride who panics on the night before her wedding," Sister Marie said gently. "You have a vocation to be a Carmelite, Sister Thérèse. Trust me. I know you." The novice director looked at Thérèse with kindness and sympathy. Raising her hand, she traced the Sign of the Cross on Thérèse's forehead. "Now go to bed and try to sleep."

"Thank you, Sister," Thérèse sighed gratefully. She left the little room with a peaceful heart.

The next morning the nuns walked in procession to the large room where Thérèse would make her vows. Suddenly thousands of swallows appeared, swooped down on the monastery, and then flew away.

For the occasion Thérèse had decorated the statue of the Child Jesus with flowers and candles. The profession of vows was private, so no guests were present. Thérèse approached Mother Marie de Gonzague and prostrated face down on the floor, a symbol of her surrender to God. Then from a slip of paper Thérèse read the promises she had written, which included this prayer: "May I never seek nor find anything or anyone but you alone, Jesus. May creatures be nothing for me and may I be nothing for them, but may you, Jesus, be everything. . . . Give me martyrdom of heart or of body, or rather give me both." At the end she prayed that her sister Leonie would receive the gift of a religious vocation and then said, "My God, I beg you, may it be your will that Papa be cured." She concluded, "May no one think of me; may I be trodden underfoot, as a little grain of sand."

Moved by seventeen-year-old Thérèse's sacrifice of love, the nuns all had tears in their eyes.

Two weeks later at a public ceremony, Thérèse was to receive her black veil. She had hoped that her father would be well enough to come just for a short while. But the day before the ceremony took place, Thérèse learned that even this was not possible. On the morning of the public ceremony, Thérèse wept. Not only would her father not be there but neither would her friend, Father Pichon. The bishop would not be present either, since he was ill.

The sisters in procession neared the chapel. To their embarrassment Thérèse was still crying. Pauline rebuked her, "I can't understand your crying. How can you hope to have Father at your ceremony?"

Mother Genevieve, the foundress of the monastery, who was too ill to attend the ceremony, even sent a note scolding Thérèse for her tears. And so this highpoint in Thérèse's life was marked by joy and sorrow.

During the following months Thérèse suffered in her heart. She had questions about her faith and doubted the goodness of her life. Gradually she learned to approach God with confidence and love. It impressed her when Mother Genevieve from her sickbed told her, "Serve God with peace and joy, Sister Thérèse. Our God is a God of peace." At this time Thérèse constantly read the writings of St. John of the Cross. She adopted as her motto his saying, "Love is repaid by love alone."

Thérèse showed love by doing her best as the assistant sacristan. Her tasks were to clean and repair the vestments and altar linens and care for the altar vessels and candles used at Mass.

She also showed love by being content with what she was given. Her habit was old and darned and didn't fit her. Her sandals too were old. Thérèse never complained. Her self-control in small matters helped her face life's greater trials. It was all part of her little way to God.

16

GOODBYES

The tolling cloister bell summoned the nuns to the infirmary. Gentle, holy Mother Genevieve was dying. For two hours Thérèse stood at the foot of her bed and prayed. It was the first time since her mother's death that Thérèse had witnessed someone die. When Mother Genevieve breathed her last breath, Thérèse felt an intense joy. She knew the holy nun was going to God. Later that night Thérèse took a piece of cloth and captured a tear that had remained on the foundress's cheek. She kept it as a precious relic.

Shortly after this, Thérèse dreamed about the foundress. In the dream Mother Genevieve gave each Carmelite something that had belonged to her. When she came to Thérèse, her hands were empty. Looking lovingly at Thérèse, she repeated three times, "To you I leave my heart."

A month later influenza struck the monastery. In those days the flu was a serious disease. All but two Carmelites became sick.

Thérèse had only a slight attack, so she cared for the sick and dying. In a few days' time, she arranged burial services for three sisters. Even Father Delatroëtte praised her courage.

Meanwhile, Mr. Martin was getting worse.

"How is Papa?" was the first question asked when Celine visited Carmel.

"Not so good," she replied. "He cries very easily and doesn't mix with others at the hospital. He just sits by himself."

"Does he realize how sick he is?" Pauline asked.

"I think he does, at least to some extent," Celine answered sadly. "He often covers his head with a handkerchief. It's as if he's embarrassed to be seen."

Marie turned to Thérèse. "That's just like the vision you saw of him when you were six, Thérèse. Do you remember?"

"Of course I do," said Thérèse. "Poor Papa," she sighed, shaking her head.

"And poor Celine," Marie added, looking at her sister through the grille. "It must be so hard for you to bear this alone."

Celine nodded. "It is," she admitted. "But I know that you are praying for us both. That and God's grace help me to bear it."

Soon Mr. Martin was sent home from the mental hospital to die. Two days later he visited Carmel in a wheelchair. He was unable to speak. As he was leaving though, he said, "In heaven." It was the last time Thérèse ever saw her father.

17

GIFTS AND TALENTS

The nuns were at recreation sewing. One drew several small pictures out of her pocket.

"Look, Sisters," she said. "Thérèse painted these. Aren't they good?"

"Let's see," said Pauline. The pictures of the saints were passed around the circle of nuns to her. As each nun examined them, she commented, "Nice," or "Lovely."

When they reached Pauline, she exclaimed, "My, these really are good! Sister Thérèse, you have talent."

"With the money we get for these cards, the rest of us will never have to work," teased one sister.

"I have an idea," said another. "Why doesn't Thérèse decorate a wall in the small prayer room?"

"Yes," someone chimed in. "She could paint the Blessed Sacrament with baby angels strewing flowers around it."

"And fluffy white clouds," added another sister.

Mother Marie de Gonzague nodded her head. "Sister Thérèse, tomorrow you will begin planning the picture for the wall. Your talent will give God praise and bring joy to all of us."

"Yes, Mother," Thérèse said, smiling. "Thank you."

"That reminds me," said an older nun with a twinkle in her eye. "Would you please write a song in honor of St. Francis, Sister Thérèse? You can just shake the words out of your sleeve. It takes me forever to put proper words to a tune."

"Certainly, Sister. I can work on it in my free time tomorrow," said Thérèse. She enjoyed writing songs and poems. They, along with her wit and cheerful disposition, added much to the community life at Carmel. If Thérèse couldn't be at recreation to entertain with her funny stories, the nuns would say, "There will be no laughing today."

A special talent Thérèse possessed was her ability to guide others in the spiritual life. This was evident in the letters she wrote to Celine. This gift was put to good use in her next assignment. When Pauline was elected prioress in 1893, she appointed Mother Marie de Gonzague novice director and Thérèse her assistant. But it was actually Thérèse who did most of the work of teaching and guiding the young sisters. Both novices, Sister Martha of Jesus and Sister Mary Magdalene, were older than Thérèse. And neither one liked her very much. Soon enough they would come to admire and love her.

18

A LITTLE WAY

Thérèse met with the two novices for talks on the spiritual life. She shared with them her ideas about God and holiness.

"We don't have to force ourselves to work hard to get to heaven," Thérèse explained. "We are ordinary people who aren't able to climb the steep stairs of perfection. We'll get to heaven not by our own efforts but by the goodness of God. The way to heaven is like taking an elevator. The elevator is the arms of God who raises us to himself. Confidence in God, that's all we need."

"But what about our sins and faults? Does God just ignore these?" Sister Martha asked.

"When we surrender ourselves to God, he accepts us as we are and loves us as we are. Even our faults can bring us closer to him, because they make us humble and help us realize that anything good in us comes from God," Thérèse replied.

"I wish I were close to God," Sister Mary Magdalene sighed. "I can't even keep awake during prayer."

"Ah," said Thérèse giving her white-veiled novice a sympathetic glance. "You have given your life to God and set apart time to pray. God loves you even when you fall asleep during prayer, just as much as a father loves his child asleep in his arms."

"Jesus did tell us to call God Father," Sister Martha commented.

"Yes," Thérèse nodded. "I can think of nothing more consoling than that. Imagine—the almighty God wants us to call him Father, Papa. That's how good and loving God is! When I can't pray, I say the Our Father very slowly."

"Sometimes I wish I could do something really great for God, like be a missionary or a martyr," Sister Mary Magdalene confided.

"Our calling is just as difficult but simple," Sister Thérèse explained. "We are to offer God all our everyday actions, thoughts, and words, all our joys and sorrows. We are to practice self-denial and hidden acts of kindness. We're not called to be great heroes, but God's little ones. We follow a little way, being humble and childlike. This is our secret. This is the easy, swift, and sure way to God."

Sister Thérèse was strict with her novices. She pointed out their faults, such as laziness or self-pity, but also asked them to point out hers. Thérèse taught most by her own example. She did the hardest work herself and practiced self-discipline. On cold laundry days she would work in cold water. She would take the place nearest the hot water on hot days. In this way another sister would have the easier job. At the laundry washtubs one sister kept splashing dirty water onto Thérèse's face. Thérèse didn't say a word. When a sister was helping her pin her habit and the pin slipped into Thérèse's shoulder, she didn't say anything. When the skin on her hands split and itched from the cold, she didn't rub them or warm them by keeping them under her long sleeves.

Thérèse called the novices her "little bunnies." She also prayed for them. The following year a third novice joined—Celine.

After five years of suffering, Mr. Martin had died, freeing Celine to accept an invitation to be a missionary in Canada or to enter the Carmelite monastery of Lisieux. One

*Thérèse did the hardest work herself
and practiced self-control.*

nun strongly opposed the entrance of another Martin. She feared that four sisters from one family would form a group and run the small community.

One day after Communion Thérèse prayed, "Jesus, you know how that sister feels about Celine's entering. If she no longer objects, I will take it as a sign that Papa is in heaven."

As the nuns were leaving the chapel, Thérèse felt a light touch on her arm. She turned to see the sister who objected to Celine's entering. "May I see you a moment?" the sister whispered.

The two stepped aside, and the older nun confided, "I've had second thoughts about Celine. She is an unusual person to have taken care of your father for so long."

"Yes," Thérèse agreed. "Celine is special. She is deeply spiritual."

"I think it best if she were to live here in Carmel where her interior life would be nurtured, don't you?"

"Definitely," Thérèse said, startled at the quick answer to her prayer.

That September Celine entered the monastery. It was Thérèse, the assistant novice director, who showed her to her cell. Celine had always been the one Thérèse looked up to during their childhood years. Now, in God's plan, the roles were reversed. Thérèse, although younger, would be Celine's teacher and guide as she began her new way of life.

19

WRITINGS

On Christmas Day the four Martin girls were together at recreation. Thérèse was entertaining her sisters by recalling some of their past Christmases. She vividly described midnight Mass, presents in the shoes, and family stories.

Suddenly, Celine exclaimed, "Mother Mary Agnes [Pauline's religious name], Sister Thérèse should really write these memories down!"

"Whatever for?" asked Thérèse in surprise. "It would be a waste of time."

"That's right," Pauline agreed. "She can always just tell us the stories. Besides, who else would be interested in them?"

Sister Marie countered, "But what if she forgets? She should get them down on paper."

"Very well," Pauline gave in with a smile. "Sister Thérèse, I'd like you to write an account of your childhood and have it to me in a year, by my feast day, January 21."

"Yes, Mother," said Thérèse. From that day on Thérèse spent her free time writing her memories in a child's notebook. She addressed the autobiography to Pauline so it has the simple, comfortable tone of someone writing to a family member.

That autumn Thérèse's flock of novices increased when her cousin Marie joined Carmel.

Then Thérèse acquired a new responsibility. A seminarian who was a missionary in Africa had sent a special request to the monastery. He was looking for a sister who would pray especially for him and the people he served. Pauline came to Thérèse while she was working at the laundry tub and showed her the letter. "Sister Thérèse," she asked, "would you be willing to become a spiritual sister to this seminarian? It would mean praying for him and writing to him."

"I'd love to!" Thérèse responded. "I've always wanted a brother who would become a priest." Through this future priest Thérèse would be able to do what she had longed to do—work in the missions.

On January 21 Thérèse handed the completed story of her childhood to Pauline. In it she compared people to flowers. She wrote, "God willed to create great souls comparable to lilies and roses, but he has also created smaller ones, and these must be content to be daisies or violets." She saw herself as a little flower. Because Pauline had a lot of business to take care of, she put the notebook into a drawer and forgot about it for two months.

In June Thérèse conceived the idea of offering her life as a sacrifice to God. In the past, people, including holy Carmelites, had offered God special sacrifices to make up for sins. Thérèse, instead, wanted to offer herself to God's love. She wanted God's love to flow through her to others.

She knocked on Pauline's door and asked, "Mother, may I please make a formal offering of myself to God as a victim to his love?" Slightly puzzled, Pauline responded, "Yes, I suppose that's all right." Thérèse wrote out her offering and asked for a priest to approve it. She chose to make her offering on the feast of the Blessed Trinity. That day at Mass, where Jesus offers himself to God the Father for us, Thérèse prayed in part, "So that my life may become an act of perfect love, I offer myself as a sacrificial victim to your merciful love, imploring you to burn me up ceaselessly and to let the floodwaters of your infinite tenderness flow into my soul, so that I may become a martyr of your love, O my God....

"O my Beloved, at every beat of my heart I want to make this offering again, an endless number of times, until the shadows fade away and I can tell you of my love face to face forever!"

Thérèse folded the paper and tucked it into her book of the Gospels.

A few days later Thérèse was in chapel praying the Stations of the Cross. She had an indescribable, supernatural experience that was both painful and sweet. She later told Pauline, "I felt myself wounded with a dart of fire. It burned so much that I thought I should die.... It seemed as if an invisible power plunged me entirely into fire. But what a fire...how sweet it was. If it had lasted a minute, even a second more, my soul would have parted from my body." This grace was a sign that God had accepted Thérèse's sacrifice. Thérèse persuaded her cousin Marie to offer herself to God's love, too.

In 1896 Mother Marie de Gonzague was elected prioress again. Thérèse had no vote in the election because of a rule that only two sisters from the same family could vote.

Mother Gonzague remained novice director in name only, while Thérèse did the work of educating the novices as usual. Mother Gonzague assigned Thérèse another task—to continue writing the story of her life. She also appointed Thérèse the spiritual sister of another missionary priest. Although Carmelites were not allowed to keep photos, Mother Gonzague instructed Thérèse, "Keep Father's photo in your writing case until I need it."

"Thank you, Mother," Thérèse said. In addition to encouraging and praising her two spiritual brothers in the letters she wrote them, Thérèse taught them her little way to God.

20

SIGNS OF TROUBLE

When Thérèse was a child, her town held a procession to honor the Body of Christ in the Blessed Sacrament. As the monstrance was carried through the streets, the children tossed rose petals along the path. Thérèse tossed hers high and loved it when they touched the monstrance.

As a nun, Thérèse strew rose petals across the feet of the crucifix in the monastery garden. The petals, a symbol of her sacrifices, showed her love for God. To her, love was the most important gift. One day she read once again the hymn in St. Paul's first letter to the Corinthians in which he also called love the greatest gift. But this time Thérèse received a new insight into her own life. "My vocation is love!" she realized. "I will *be* love!"

Thérèse sensed that she did not have many years left to be love on earth. One night she dreamed that she was walking in a hall. There she met three Carmelites from heaven clothed in mantles and veils. Thérèse thought, *How happy I would be if I could see one of their faces.* With that, the tallest saint came forward. Thérèse fell to her knees, and the saint lifted her veil, covered Thérèse with it, and embraced her. Immediately Thérèse knew she was Mother Anne of Jesus, the founder of Carmel in France.

"Mother, I beg you, tell me if God will leave me much longer on earth. Will he send for me soon?" Thérèse asked.

"Yes, soon, very soon. I promise you," Blessed Anne replied.

"Mother," Thérèse continued, "tell me also if God requires more of me than I have been able to do? Is he happy with me?"

Mother Anne's face became more radiant. She replied tenderly, "God asks nothing more of you. He is very pleased." Then she took Thérèse's head between her hands and kissed her. Thérèse was about to ask for favors for her sisters when she woke up.

Before going to heaven, however, Thérèse would have much suffering to offer God. It all began on Holy Thursday, the evening on which the Church recalls the Last Supper and Jesus' agony in the garden. Some of the nuns spent all that night of 1896 praying before the Blessed Sacrament. Thérèse was sent to bed at midnight. The next morning she knew she had to report to the prioress what had happened during the night. It was something she welcomed with joy because she thought she was dying.

After prayers, she went to Mother Marie de Gonzague and knelt as the sisters did when speaking to the prioress.

"Mother," Thérèse began, "last night I coughed up blood. I spat it into a handkerchief and then was able to sleep soundly. May I continue the lenten practices?"

"How do you feel now?" Mother Marie de Gonzague asked with concern.

"I feel fine," Thérèse replied. "It was nothing. I have no pain. Please let me go on with the lenten prayers and fasting."

"All right, Sister," the prioress agreed, "since there are only two days left until Easter."

So Thérèse continued the lenten fast, which on that day, Good Friday, meant a meal of only bread and water.

That afternoon, after the long prayers in chapel, Thérèse was washing windows in the cold hall. A novice walked by and noticed how pale and faint she looked.

"Sister Thérèse, please let me finish these windows for you," the novice offered.

"Thank you, Sister, but I'm almost done. I'm sure you have your own work to do." Thérèse replied, sending the novice away.

That night Thérèse again spat up blood. She didn't light her lamp to check her handkerchief, but slept until morning.

After Easter, the doctor was called to the monastery. He "examined" Thérèse by putting his head through the small opening of the chapel grille through which the nuns received Communion. He prescribed some medicine for her throat and left things at that.

In the summer, Thérèse developed a cough. Again the doctor said, "It's nothing serious. I suggest that she be served better food. Let her eat meat." Thérèse was served meat. The cough disappeared, and the nuns even considered transferring Thérèse to a Carmelite monastery in China for which she had volunteered.

But it was not to be.

21

A HAPPY SUFFERER

That winter Thérèse suffered from one fever after another. In spite of this, she followed all the Carmelite customs of prayer and fasting when Lent came again. Her cough became constant and her fever never seemed to leave. Nights were a long nightmare of shivering and painful coughing spasms. The doctor tried various treatments: hot plasters, which blistered the skin, massages, and hot needles inserted hundreds of times into her back. At that time, people were just learning about tuberculosis, a disease that destroys the lungs and leads to suffocation. There was no cure for it, and in its early stages it was difficult to diagnose. It was a long time before Thérèse's doctor realized that she had TB.

During this time, Thérèse lived the full schedule of the Carmelites, including all the work and prayers. She helped out in the sacristy, a duty which she loved. In her free time she would even stop by to see if the sister in charge needed help.

Thérèse only grew weaker. She walked through the halls and up the stairs slowly, leaning on the wall. When she could no longer eat, she was relieved of all work except one—that of finishing her autobiography.

"Sister Thérèse, how are you today?" a sister greeted. Thérèse was sitting in the garden in her father's wheelchair, writing.

"I can't complain," Thérèse answered, flashing her visitor a smile. "How are you?"

"Fine," the nun replied, shifting a pitchfork from one shoulder to the next. She was only one of several sisters who would stop to chatter about hay, the ducks, and a hundred other unimportant matters. Thérèse never showed impatience at the many interruptions. But this type of hidden heroism was not understood by all.

Once, through the window of her cell, Thérèse heard the sisters talking in the kitchen. One said, "Well, Sister Thérèse is going to die soon. I wonder what the prioress will find to say about her after her death. Sister Thérèse is very nice, but she's never done anything worth talking about."

Thérèse wrote the last chapters of her autobiography with great effort. In the end, she used a pencil because dipping a pen in ink was too exhausting. The last passage Thérèse wrote was an appeal to have confidence in God. She said that even if she had on her conscience every crime that could be committed, she would still throw herself into the arms of her Savior. Because of his love and mercy she wrote, "I know that all that multitude of sins would disappear in an instant, as a drop of water cast into a flaming furnace." In reality she could claim, "Since the age of three I have refused God nothing." Thérèse handed her manuscript to the prioress at the beginning of July.

That month Thérèse brought up a flow of blood several times. Eventually she was carried from her cell that she loved down to the infirmary. Mother Marie de Gonzague appointed Celine as assistant in the infirmary and entrusted her with the care of her sister. Pauline came often to talk with Thérèse and recorded their conversations in a notebook.

Thérèse suffered intensely for weeks. Besides coughing up blood, she had a hard time breathing and could barely eat or drink. Despite her pain, Thérèse teased, joked, and made her visitors laugh. She wrote letters to her spiritual brothers and tried to cheer them up about her condition.

But Thérèse also became deeply depressed and had temptations about her faith. She described it by saying, "I feel as though I'm in a dark tunnel." She assured everyone, though, that she was at peace.

At the end of the month, Thérèse received the Anointing of the Sick. She explained to Pauline, "I know I'm going to die soon, but when? I can't tell. I am like a child that's always promised a cake. He sees it far off, then when he goes near to take it, the hand draws back! But I am perfectly prepared to live or die."

One day Thérèse and Pauline spoke about her writings. Pauline said, "The best way to teach others your little way to God will be by publishing what you've written about your life."

"That's right," Thérèse agreed. "After my death you mustn't speak to anyone except Mother Prioress about my manuscript before it is published. It's a very important work, but there will be difficulties in getting it printed."

Pauline asked Thérèse to reread her manuscript to see if she wanted to change anything. When Thérèse finished reading, she made a kind of prophecy. "These pages will do a great deal of good," she said simply. "They will make God's loving-kindness better known. I feel that all the world is going to love me."

For a few days Thérèse seemed to be better and was hungry. She even asked Celine for a chocolate éclair! Otherwise, Thérèse ate mush. At one time, although she didn't like milk, the doctor put her on a milk diet. This was worse to her than the painful treatments.

On August 6, the Feast of the Transfiguration, Thérèse struggled all night with temptations to doubt God's goodness. She prayed, looking at a picture of the Holy Face of Jesus, which hung by her bed above a nightlight.

Her confidence in God won out.

22

FINAL DAYS

In mid-August the doctor said, "Sister Thérèse's lungs are so bad that she can't live more than a few days." Despite that prediction, she suffered six more weeks with terrible pain in her sides and stomach.

"What this patient is going through is frightful," the amazed doctor declared to Mother Marie de Gonzague, "yet she has the face of an angel. I've never seen that before in others who suffer so much."

One day, Celine, with tears in her eyes, said to Thérèse, "I have prayed that you wouldn't have to suffer so much, and now you're suffering terribly."

Thérèse replied, "I have prayed to God not to listen to any prayers which would set obstacles in the way of the fulfillment of his will with regard to me. God has always helped me, leading me by the hand since my childhood, and I rely upon him now. Even though I have to go through the worst, I know he will be there with me."

"What do you say to God when you spend these long nights praying?" Celine asked Thérèse one sleepless night.

Thérèse responded, "I say nothing. I just love him."

The nuns who came to visit asked her questions.

"Thérèse, would you rather die or get well?"

"As God wills," Thérèse would respond.

"Will you die on a feast day?" another asked.

"My death will be a feast day enough for me," answered Thérèse with a smile. In fact, Thérèse smiled so much that some sisters doubted that she was sick.

Thérèse often repeated, "You will see. After my death I will let fall a shower of roses." By this she promised that she would ask God for graces and favors to send to those on earth. She looked forward to her death because, as she explained, "I feel that my mission is soon to begin, to make others love God as I do, to teach others my 'little way.' I will spend my heaven in doing good upon earth."

"Will you look down upon us from heaven?" the sisters pleaded.

"I say nothing. I just love him."

"No," Thérèse surprised them. "I will come down!"

One day Celine remarked, "To think that the sisters in our Carmel mission in China still think you will be coming."

Thérèse replied, "I will come to them soon. If you only knew how swiftly I shall make my rounds, once I am in heaven. I will help little children receive baptism, I will assist priests, missionaries, the whole Church."

On September 14, the Feast of the Holy Cross, Thérèse was given a rose. She plucked the petals and let them fall on her crucifix. Some petals dropped on the floor. "Be sure you pick up those petals," Thérèse instructed, "They will give pleasure later." The sisters saved the rose petals. Thirteen years later a cancer patient was instantly cured by touching one of them.

Because of her disease, Thérèse could not receive Communion in her final weeks. Someone asked, "Won't it bother you not to be able to receive the Eucharist on the day you die?"

"No," Thérèse answered simply. "Everything is grace."

Although Thérèse's body was wasting away, her face radiated peace and joy. She commented to Pauline, "I long for the great crossing over. I am like a traveler, exhausted and harried, who collapses when he reaches his destination. But I fall into the arms of God."

The day before Thérèse died, Celine asked her, "Before you leave, give us parting words to remember."

Thérèse responded, "I have said all I have to say. All is accomplished. It is love alone that counts."

On September 30, 1897, Thérèse was suffering intensely. About three o'clock in the afternoon, she spread her arms open like Jesus on the cross. She turned to Mother Marie de Gonzague. "Oh, Mother," she begged, "present me quickly to the Blessed Virgin. Help me to die well."

Mother Marie de Gonzague replied softly, "You are ready to appear before your judge. You have understood and practiced humility."

Thérèse then repeated several times, "I do not regret having given myself up to love."

That evening, with the prioress and Thérèse's three sisters around her bed, Thérèse looked at her crucifix. "Oh, I love him! My God, I love you!" she murmured. Then her head fell back on the pillow.

"Open all the doors," Mother Marie de Gonzague ordered.

A bell summoned all the sisters to Thérèse's room. As they knelt around her bed, Thérèse opened her eyes and stared above them. She looked radiantly happy. Then she closed her eyes and exhaled her last breath. Her face became as white and glowing as a fresh lily. She was only twenty-four years old.

Now that Thérèse had gone to heaven, her work on earth was about to begin, as she had predicted.

23

A Shower of Roses

Thérèse was buried in the Carmelite section of the public cemetery in Lisieux. A simple cross marked her grave. It was inscribed with the words, "I will spend my heaven in doing good upon earth."

A year later the bishop gave permission to publish her autobiography, *The Story of a Soul*. Two thousand copies were printed. Celine painted a portrait of Thérèse, which was published in the book. By 1915 the book had been translated into thirty-five languages. People were fascinated by Thérèse's life and her little way. Under Celine's supervision, the sisters sent out millions of pictures of her and thousands of relics, pieces of objects she had used. Each day the sisters received numerous letters. Women flocked to Carmelite monasteries asking to be admitted as postulants.

Although Thérèse had not worked miracles on earth, true to her word, she now flooded the world with "roses." People from all walks of life asked her to intercede with

God for them for all kinds of favors, and their requests were granted. The sick, the paralyzed, and those suffering mentally were healed. Missionaries were helped. Sinners were converted. Lisieux became a place of pilgrimage. Before long, popular pressure encouraged Rome to begin the process of canonization, declaring Thérèse a saint. This process was slowed by World War I, during which soldiers looked to Thérèse for protection, even naming their planes after her.

In 1925 the Church officially declared Thérèse a saint. For her canonization, the pope, for the first time in more than fifty years, ordered that St. Peter's Basilica be outlined with torches and lamps. Three hundred workers saw that the dome was lit that night. All four of Thérèse's sisters were alive to see her canonized.

Later Thérèse was named patroness of France along with St. Joan of Arc. Thérèse, with St. Francis of Xavier, is also the patron of foreign missionaries.

In 1997, a hundred years after Thérèse's death, the Church declared her a Doctor of the Church. This title is given to experts in theology. At that time only two women were doctors: St. Teresa of Avila and St. Catherine of Siena.

In the chapel of Carmel is a statue of St. Thérèse. Beneath it is a casket containing her relics. Above Thérèse's relics is the statue of Mary that smiled on her when she was ten.

In 2002 Thérèse's relics were taken to many countries, including Iraq, on a pilgrimage of peace.

Yes, Thérèse sends us roses, but her greatest gift is her little way. This Saint of the Possible showed us how anyone can become a saint. *All it takes is love.*

PRAYER

Saint Thérèse, your love for Jesus led you to try to do every little thing well. By being hidden, small, and totally open to what God wanted, you became a powerful saint.

Teach me to live your way of love too. Help me to treat everyone kindly, to be patient, to pray for people who are away from God, and to accept things that are hard or make me suffer. Let me follow this way with determination and cheerfulness. Then someday I will be with you in our Father's home. Amen.

GLOSSARY

1. **Anointing of the Sick**—the sacrament by which Jesus gives spiritual comfort and strength, and sometimes physical help to someone who is dangerously ill.

2. **Basilica**—an important, usually large church.

3. **Chaplain**—a priest who ministers to a certain group, such as at a school or prison.

4. **Cloister**—the area where members of certain religious orders live; other people are not allowed in it.

5. **Consecrate**—to set aside a person or an object for God and God's service.

6. **Conversion**—a change of heart, usually describing a sinner's repentance.

7. **Divine Office**—the official prayer of the Church containing psalms and Scripture readings that is prayed several times a day.

8. **Foundress**—a woman who begins a religious community.

9. **Habit**—the clothing that identifies a priest, brother or sister as a member of a religious community.

10. **Infirmary**—a place where the sick are cared for.

11. **Memorare**—a popular prayer to Mary for help.

12. **Monastery**—the place where monks or nuns live, dedicating themselves to a life of prayer.

13. **Monstrance**—the sacred vessel (container) that allows the Blessed Sacrament to be seen for adoration.

14. **Novena**—praying a prayer for nine days, hours or months.

15. **Novice**—a person in the special period of training that comes before the making of vows in religious life.

16. **Pentecost**—the feast fifty days after Easter when we celebrate the coming of the Holy Spirit to the Church.

17. **Pilgrimage**—a journey to a holy place to honor God.

18. **Postulant**—a person taking first steps in religious life; a candidate.

19. **Poverty**—giving up material goods for the sake of being closer to God.

20. **Retreat**—a period of prayer and silence for renewing one's spiritual life

21. **Prioress**—the head of a monastery.

22. **Rosary**—a prayer in which we think about events in the lives of Jesus and Mary while saying Our Fathers, Hail Marys and Glory Bes on a circle of beads.

23. **Sacrifice**—a gift offered to God, such as something difficult that we do.

24. **Sacristan**—a person who takes care of the sacred vessels, vestments, and various articles used in church.

25. **Vocation**—a call from God to a certain lifestyle. A person may have a vocation to the married life, the priesthood, the religious life, or the single life. Everyone has a vocation to be holy.

26. **Vow**—a solemn promise made to God. Religious priests, brothers and sisters usually make vows of poverty, chastity, and obedience.

BOOKS & MEDIA

The Daughters of St. Paul operate book and media centers at the following addresses. Visit, call or write the one nearest you today, or find us on the World Wide Web, www. pauline.org

CALIFORNIA
3908 Sepulveda Blvd, Culver City, CA 90230	310-397-8676
2640 Broadway Street, Redwood City, CA 94063	650-369-4230
5945 Balboa Avenue, San Diego, CA 92111	858-565-9181

FLORIDA
145 S.W. 107th Avenue, Miami, FL 33174	305-559-6715

HAWAII
1143 Bishop Street, Honolulu, HI 96813	808-521-2731
Neighbor Islands call:	800-259-8463

ILLINOIS
172 North Michigan Avenue, Chicago, IL 60601	312-346-4228

LOUISIANA
4403 Veterans Memorial Blvd, Metairie, LA 70006	504-887-7631

MASSACHUSETTS
885 Providence Hwy Dedham, MA 02026	781-326-5385

MISSOURI
9804 Watson Road, St. Louis, MO 63126	314-965-3512

NEW JERSEY
561 U.S. Route 1, Wick Plaza, Edison, NJ 08817	732-572-1200

NEW YORK
Relocating. Please call:	212-754-1110

PENNSYLVANIA
9171-A Roosevelt Blvd, Philadelphia, PA 19114	215-676-9494

SOUTH CAROLINA
243 King Street, Charleston, SC 29401	843-577-0175

VIRGINIA
1025 King Street, Alexandria, VA 22314	703-549-3806

CANADA
3022 Dufferin Street, Toronto, Ontario, Canada M6B 3T5	416-781-9131

¡También somos su fuente para libros, videos y música en español!